Don’t Panic!

by

Robert W. Krepps

Double 9 BOOKS

Don't Panic!

by Robert W. Krepps

ISBN: 978-93-68097-98-3

Published by

DOUBLE 9 BOOKS
2/13-B, Ansari Road
Daryaganj, New Delhi – 110002
info@double9books.com
www.double9books.com
Tel. 011-40042856

ABOUT THE AUTHOR

Robert W. Krepps was a prolific author known for his contributions to science fiction, historical fiction, and fantasy. His works often explore complex themes such as human resilience, societal breakdown, and the emotional depth of his characters. Krepps' writing blends speculative elements with philosophical insights, offering readers a reflection on humanity's survival instinct in the face of crisis. Some of his most notable works include Don't Panic!, a practical guide for managing life's challenges, and El Cid, a historical novel based on the legendary Spanish hero. Krepps also wrote Vengeance from the Past, Tomorrow the World!, and Sinbad: Through Time and Space, among others. His stories often blend adventure with deeper psychological themes, exploring fantastical worlds that reveal the complexities of the human condition. Krepps made lasting contributions to 20th-century speculative fiction, blending imagination with thoughtful explorations of survival, loss, and personal growth. His work resonates with readers who appreciate his unique blend of adventure and introspection.

CONTENTS

Despite conflicting reports, the Air Force believed in the flying saucers. The scares began in 1947 and as a responsible agency the Air Force had to start investigations. At various times they'd cautiously release some information; then there would be some hysteria and they'd hurriedly debunk the whole business as "mass hallucinations" and "crackpot theories" until the public had regained its balance, when they'd start letting out bits of truth once more. The nature and implications of the saucer sightings made this on-again-off-again policy necessary in dealing with such an unstable thing as a war-nervous, tensed-up population. If the truth about the saucers had been known, the entire truth, then the Air Force could have published it and the country would have accepted it in stride; but the mystery that clouded the strange ships was susceptible of too many interpretations.

In December of 1952 a blue-lighted saucer was sighted, without a shadow of a doubt, over Laredo, Texas. In January of '53 a whole V-formation of blue objects appeared over Santa Ana, California. These were military sightings and beyond question. There were many before and even more afterward. Some of them mentioned blue lights and some other colors, and the daylight viewings talked of silver metallic luster.

The first low-flying saucer to be reported authoritatively was that which flew over the Capitol in Washington at 11:18 a.m. on Saturday, Christmas Day, 1954. It was caught by the cameras that were making a telecast at that time of the festivities in Washington, and beamed without explanation all over the country. A few minutes later the screens of America's viewers went blank and then the President appeared to urge calmness and sanity. There was no question of mass hallucination and crackpot theories any longer. The saucer was perhaps three hundred feet broad; it was of the usual shape reported in previous sightings, round with a central cabin, and it was green in color. It had flown comparatively slowly, at an estimated 125 m.p.h. It had disappeared over the Potomac.

At 2:24 p.m. the President was on tv again. There was some commotion at the door of the room from which he was broadcasting. He turned his head and nearly one hundred million people who were jammed before television sets across the nation saw his jaw drop and his eyes bulge slightly with irrepressible awe. In about nine seconds a very curious group walked into camera range. There were half a dozen secret service men with drawn guns, and in their midst, the target of those watchful weapons, was the first of the green horde.

He was—the measurements were determined later—six feet seven and one-half inches tall. He was dressed in a green shirt and trousers, caught around the waist by a heavy belt on which were stitched a number of cabalistic designs; on the left breast were more of the same, a circle and three slim triangles. In a holster slung at the right side of his belt was a large revolver or pistol. It was what had been known in the old West as a half-breed holster, enabling the wearer to swing up the muzzle and fire the gun without jerking it free of the leather. The alien had his hands folded carefully across his chest. Had he made a single motion toward the gun, he would have been blown in two.

In proportions and frame he was very like a human being. His chest was deep and his legs and arms well muscled. His skin was a delicate, olive-green in hue, as those viewers with color tv could see. His face was normal, perhaps a bit stern in expression, but with the ordinary features of a man, except that he had only one eye. It was located immediately above the bridge of his nose; it was about four times the area of a human eye and almost round in shape, and its small pupil roamed swiftly to and fro as the alien walked slowly toward the President. The pupil of the eye was like a tiny animal in a cage, dashing from side to side, up and down, uncanny, incredible, and horrifying.

The cameras did not show his feet. These were somewhat like those of an ostrich, each having two enormous toes, naked, horny, and padded with thick layers of green fatty matter on the soles.

The tint of his skin could have been accepted as a mutation of the strictly human animal. The single eye, even, might have suggested a humanoid sport or far-future development. But the feet were utterly inhuman and even the most callous or most unimaginative among the citizens who saw him personally that first day agreed that the feet were terrifying.

The cameras were turned off after about twenty seconds. An announcer came on and spluttered some drivel about keeping cool and not losing our heads, spoiling the effect of these admonitions at once by a piercing, hysterical giggle.

Before a quarter of an hour had elapsed, there were minor riots and demonstrations throughout the continent. The worst of these were sparked by fanatic groups claiming that the end of the world had come. Others, scarcely less violent, went screaming that the Martians were invading us, that the White House had been captured "right on the television" and much more of such idiocies. In many places the militia were called out to suppress waves of looting and street fighting.

The Air Force, which had not been taken entirely unaware, since they had privately come to the conclusion some time before that the flying saucers were extraterrestrial, now flung a canopy of fighter planes, both jet and motor-driven, over Washington, and, somewhat later, Pittsburgh, Detroit, Birmingham and New York. Chicago, Los Angeles, and other cities of strategic importance were likewise protected within a period of two hours.

The rioting was subdued by evening. Army trucks equipped with public address systems patrolled everywhere, repeating the warnings to keep calm and do nothing until official word was broadcast of our intentions toward the aliens and vice versa. Meanwhile the first of the green horde was given a comfortable room in the Pentagon, where he was kept under an unobtrusive but thorough twenty-four-hour-a-day guard, and where means of communication with him were speedily sought for.

In a matter of a day and a half, or, to be precise, at two minutes to midnight on Sunday the 26th of December, he articulated his first English word. It was "Yes." Shortly he proved that he had absorbed much more than this word, for he began making attempts at complete sentences around 2:00 a.m. on the 27th. He had been under the constant supervision and teaching of a corps of scientists, language experts, and assorted brain-workers; he had shown no desire for sleep during the thirty-six hours he had been on the ground, and had listened to and worked with the teachers all that time. He showed now a good rudimentary grasp of English. It was given as the official opinion that he had shown in this the intelligence of a human genius, although not of the very highest order, rating perhaps an I.Q. of 195.

In the eight-hour period following this he spoke with the President and assured him, partly in words and partly in signs, that the folk of the green saucers were friendly explorers from a distant galaxy. His voice was throaty and rather unpleasant, with a tendency to crack in the upper registers.

He expressed a desire to return to his saucer for some purpose which he could not make plain with his basic English. This was at 10:17 a.m. on the 27th. It was considered politic to allow him to enter the saucer alone. He did so, by a method which was unfortunately not communicated to the public later. Shortly the craft rose from the earth and shot rapidly out of sight in the direction of Mount Vernon. There was no jet exhaust detected in its take-off; it simply rose like an iron filing to a magnet, soundless and abrupt. For three days thereafter there were no reported sightings of saucers.

It was officially decided in this period that the green man with the single eye and bird's feet was not intent on mischief; he had been given an idea of how far we had progressed technically, in many fields, but the information was only what he and his kind could have discovered for themselves in the years'-long surveillance of the world which they must have been making. No secrets had been imparted to him and he had expressed nothing but cordiality and good will, though he had managed to tell the interrogators only a little about himself and his race and home planet, which when boiled down and analyzed came to this: his home was far away (of course it would be) and he was friendly.

After the three-day lapse, saucers were detected on radar screens all over the civilized world: rather too high for the usual reconnaissance, they came and passed in greater numbers than ever before. No planes reported them, their altitude being too great. This long-distance traffic worried the governments of every nation. It was capable of so many explanations that deduction was futile. The protective canopies of fighter planes remained over key cities in the United States and Canada, and to some extent over the capitals and industrial centers of the world.

Eight days after the tremendous influx of saucers, Russia issued her considered opinion. The green one-eyed man was a capitalistic hoax. No such creature existed. The radar blips were "a" natural phenomenon, "b" a secret weapon of the Soviet, "c" a secret weapon of America and or Britain, "d" a capitalistic hoax. Somehow the masters of propaganda made it appear that all four of these silly charges were true, notwithstanding their mutual cancellation.

Two days thereafter the green horde launched its attack, at 11:34 a.m. on Sunday, the 9th of January, 1955.

CHAPTER II

Although the great flights of fighter planes were continually aloft, the reassuring program had gone on, the broadcasting trucks still rumbling about the streets foghorning their messages of cheer and optimism to a somewhat restive public. Some elements of the free press had been warning direly of "unknown dangers" and "possible treachery"—this causing some gimlet-eyed gentlemen in high places to come out with bills and demands for suppression of a free press for the duration of the so-called negotiations with the alien people. There had been no negotiations whatever. In this case, as in many others, the free press was perfectly right; but their warnings in the face of official hopefulness served only to confuse and fret the public. Hence, the tv lulled, the radio allayed, and the bellowing loudspeakers on the cruising trucks attempted to quiet fear under a blanket of sound.

At the said moment of attack, 11:34 a.m., the green saucers swept down with a perfection of simultaneity that made you think, as someone said later, that the devil had murmured "Synchronize your watches, boys." They hurtled from the skies over New York and Bangkok and Berlin and London and Madrid and Shanghai, down upon Moscow and San Francisco and Tokyo and Paris and Bombay. In the instant that the devastation hit New Orleans it also smashed at Edinburgh and Nome and Minsk and Berne. The first skyscraper toppled in Chicago as the first factory blew to flinders in Rio de Janeiro.

It was curious that their weapons did not seem to include the atomic variety. No A-bombs or H-bombs; rays, of incalculable destructive power and unknown origin, lanced from the diving saucers and struck the earth with the force of exploding bombs, but instead of crashing and then echoing away, these explosions continued, like great rolls of terrible thunder, for as long as the rays were aimed downward. One ray, directed from the belly-port of a canting ship, would set the ground a-shudder, crumple all structures in its path or near it, and create an ear-shattering blast that kept on and on until the saucer, tilting away, shut off the ray. So that each ray, in effect, was like an unending and ever-replenished series of huge bombs—and from each ship came a ray, and over each city there were hundreds of ships....

The mighty centers of civilization were obliterated. The great concentrations of population over the globe died. Manufacturing cities and cities which produced nothing of strategic value whatever were smeared indiscriminately into blood and dust and muck. It was an attack, not at man's weapons or production, but at man himself. It was the beginning of man's end, a giant step toward his classification with the dodo, the auk, the sabertooth tiger and the passenger pigeon.

One large eastern city in the United States presented a typical picture during that hour of cataclysm. In the first fifteen minutes its canopy of fighter planes was blown out of the sky; the weapons they carried, some of them atomic, were as effective against the green saucers as sling-shots on platinum. By noon the air had begun to fill with billowing, drifting masses of smoke-yellow vapor, reeking of sulphur and molten metal and burnt flesh and death. Those who had been unlucky enough to live through the attack thus far were now so nauseated by the odors of mankind's collapse that they stumbled among the shattering streets, retching and vomiting, as eager to escape the yellow hell-cloud's stink as they were to avoid the crumbling steel and cement.

At the end of an hour, while the greater part of the two hundred and twenty-eight saucers continued to raze the city, one alien ship made a landing on a leveled field of the suburbs. Its entry port jawed open, somewhat like a huge clamshell parting, and a single green man emerged. He was six feet nine and his eye measured a good four inches across. He carried a flag of red, white and green, on which the device of a circle and three triangles which he wore on his left breast was repeated. He strode away from the ship, gazing about with satisfaction. Some distance off lay the wreckage of a broadcasting truck; its warped, ruined loudspeakers yawned over the body of an Army sergeant, who still held in a firm grip the microphone into which he had been talking when the world was scuttled around him.

On the side of the demolished truck there remained a sign which read DON'T PANIC—THEY'RE FRIENDLY!

There was blood on the sergeant's mouth and forehead and he had bled from the nose. The blood was almost wholly dry now. His eyes were open.

The green conqueror looked at him and grinned. It remains one of the most curious facts of the matter that both mankind and the bird-footed beasts of the green horde expressed amusement and pleasure by turning up the corners of the mouth....

The alien peered all about him, shading his eye with his right hand. Nothing moved anywhere except the skimming saucers and the collapsing city. He stepped forward and lifted his pennon high, to plant its ten-foot staff in the dead body of the earthman. Holding it up, he spoke a few words in his own language, a guttural cracking speech which ranged up and down like that of an excited bird.

As he was about to stab the corpse with his flag, the corpse rolled onto its back and contracted its body, shot up its feet and kicked the alien square in the belly.

Catching the shaft of the flag, the erstwhile dead sergeant jerked it out of the alien's grasp, immediately bounded to his feet, took a firm two-handed grip of the thing—the sharp lance-head made it a splendid weapon—and ran it with savage violence straight into the throat of the green man, who died instantly and without sound.

Pausing only to shake his head once, because it ached fiercely, the sergeant bent over the tall body, folded one big hand around the pistol and its half-breed holster, and yanked. The retaining strap broke. The sergeant turned and began to run in the opposite direction from the grounded saucer, which continued to show no sign of life. Shortly he had disappeared into the smoking, burning ruins of the city's edge.

And so at 12:46 p.m. on January 9th, 1955, a moribund world drew the first blood from its extraterrestrial assassins.

CHAPTER III

Trace Roscoe had been a sergeant, off and on, for nine years. He belonged to the regular Army and had never thought of choosing any other career. Twice he had been busted to corporal and twice regained his stripes. Once he had been up for a commission and had, after due thought, refused it, because he'd known he wouldn't have it long. He had an Irish temper, and that was from his mother; he had a bulldog English muddle-through determination, and that was from his father. He was a hell of a good man in a fight. He was the best driver in his company, a better mechanic than a driver, and a better boxer than either. He read adventure novels and Von Clausewitz and Spillane and Voltaire and anything else that happened his way. He didn't consider himself much of a brain, but would have smeared the man who implied he was less intelligent than Einstein, for a man's opinion of himself should not be held by other people.

He had been driving his broadcasting truck along Highwood Avenue when the saucers attacked. He had been reciting the pap about not panicking, and hoping that he could personally see one of the single-eyed aliens sometime. He put no faith in the friendly-explorer crud. He wanted to look into that lone eye and decide for himself what the critters intended, because Trace Roscoe fancied himself a pretty good judge of character, even the character of ostrich-hoofed schmoes from outer space.

Well, the earth rose up around him and his truck before he rightly knew what was going on; and after a period of blackness he woke up to pain and a stench like one of Poe's charnel houses in his nostrils. He found that he was lying with his left arm draped over a jagged hunk of truck, clutching the mike with stiff fingers. Not being one to act without thinking in an emergency, he lay perfectly quiet and listened for a while to the rumble and crump of bombs—which he later found out had been the rays from the saucers instead—and the buzzing of his own skull. He could taste blood and feel it drying on his skin. He didn't believe he was at all badly hurt.

A little way from his face there was a busted headlight. He gazed at it a while, collecting his thoughts and opinions, and noticing that an arrangement of the shattered glass and chrome made a quite respectable mirror in which he could see a good deal of what went on behind him. Before he had decided what to do, he saw the saucer come to ground on the blasted field. He played possum and after a bit he saw the greenie come up the rise and stand there glaring around, holding the queer pennon and tipping back the pronged helmet from his eye.

Trace concentrated on holding still until the critter stepped over to him, and then Trace exploded all over the poor bastard, and took away his gun, which he wouldn't be needing any longer, and ran.

He half expected to be popped off by a bullet or a ray or a lord-knew-what from the saucer, but he reached the first edge of ruins safely and went to ground like a rabbit. Sitting in an angle of broken wall, he scanned the city. The saucers were engaged in a final mop-up. Trace felt sick. He looked at his town from end to end and he knew there couldn't be a dozen people alive in it. He had no way of knowing what was happening to the rest of the world, but he made some shrewd guesses. He was aware of the incredible number of blips that had been showing up on the radar screens lately. He knew that this city wasn't important enough in the scheme of things to warrant more than a small section of the attacking forces. This must be what Revelations called "the great day of God" when good and evil fought it out at Armageddon. Except that evil seemed to be winning, hands down.

Trace Roscoe peeked over his wall at the grounded saucer, and saw that a lot of greenies were coming out of it, advancing cautiously toward their dead comrade who lay with ten feet of flag-pole sticking up from his throat. Trace counted them as an automatic action (there were seventeen), in case he would need to know how many made up a saucer's crew in the future. Then he bent low and ran from hillock to hillock through what had that morning been the south-western suburbs of his city. As he ran he discarded the holster of the alien's gun, and thrust the weapon itself into his belt. If he had had a few minutes to examine it, and had he discovered how many loads it carried, he would have remained and started a fight with the one-eyers. Running was strategically correct in view of his ignorance of his only weapon.

When he had covered a mile he got up on a one-story-high mound of rubble and looked back. The green men had planted their flag and returned to their craft; even as Trace watched, it rose like a round green bullet and disappeared above the yellow haze. None of the other saucers landed, so far as he could see. The landing, then, had been for the vainglorious purpose of leaving their banner in token of victory. Trace spat and jumped down and went on into the city.

The reek made him gag now and then, but he had smelled some god-awful things in his time and was able to control his uneasy stomach. He considered the possibility of poison gas and judged it too slight to worry over; the destroying rays had certainly no need of accompanying gases, for they were as all-destructive as a thousand hurricanes rolled up in one package.

By three o'clock—his watch, miraculously, was still going—Trace had entered the city itself. He trotted down a broken, heaped-up thoroughfare, his glance roving constantly from side to side in search of movement. A sergeant whose army was gone had to find himself another in a hurry; and if so be it he was the general in that one, well, Trace Roscoe was ready to take on the job.

He had no fanatical hope of beating the greenies, because he was a soldier and level-headed, and odds of some millions to one were no odds at all. He figured the enemy's strength at something between ten and a hundred thousand saucers, with at least twenty individuals crewing each. There were at a conservative estimate 200,000 troops on the other side; and more like 2,000,000. So Trace was not indulging in any optimism when he started hunting for an army. He was merely following his natural inclinations, which were to fight the opposition as long as he had breath in his body and hands on the ends of his arms.

He was not full of sorrow and wild regret either, for that wasn't Trace's way. Besides which, the destruction of the civilization of this earth was too big to be grasped and understood all at once. If Trace had found the bodies of a score of people, he might have burst into tears, for his heart was big and Irish and sentimental. But pacing down the stinking tomb of hundreds of thousands of men and women was so incredible as to be simply a fact and not a comprehensible horror.

Alone he stood in the middle of a more-or-less flat plain in the city, staring and listening; and when he heard the shout, he went toward it at once, exulting that so quickly he'd discovered a private, or it might be a captain, for his army. There was a hole that was floored with cracked steps and went down into the ground, and Trace dived into it without hesitation.

Sitting at the bottom, with chunks of concrete heaped around him like divot around a duffer's tee, was a thin gentleman in a mustache, half a top hat, one leg of a pair of black trousers, and little else but a scowl. "They killed her," he said as Trace came into his view. "They blew her right out of my arms."

"Can you stand?" Trace asked him, reaching out one big hand.

"I don't know. Ouch! Yes, I can," said the man. "I tell you, they murdered Fannie."

"I'm sorry, fellow. Your wife?"

"My rabbit."

"Rabbit?" Trace turned him around and looked him over for wounds; there were none more serious than extensive bruises.

"I'm a magician," said the naked man. "Blacknight the Great. I had Fannie for three years and she never made a mistake. Smartest damn rabbit you ever saw. I was carrying her to a shelter and one of those rays shot along over the Farinello Building and the whole street blew up and she was gone, just like that. Damn green monsters." He stared at the sergeant. "I suppose it seems silly to you, feeling bad about a rabbit?"

"No," Trace said shortly. "I had a marmoset once. Let's get out of here and see how many others are alive."

"I haven't heard a thing for an hour," Blacknight said. "Not until your footsteps in the gravel. I think they're all gone." The two men stood in the open, craning their necks. "Nobody," the thin man said bitterly. "Two men left out of a world. We can't even start our race again. That takes a female too. My God," he said suddenly, and put his hands over his face.

"Come on," Trace Roscoe said sharply. "I'm hungry."

The naked magician looked up at him. "In the middle of this?" he said, and then, considering, "I guess I am too. I wouldn't have thought it was possible."

Farther along they found the remains of a two-story department store; a lot of it was gone, but in the mess they managed to find a shirt and a pair of pants for Bill Blacknight—he swore it was his own name—and a couple of cans of corned beef hash. They invented a skillet and stove out of twisted metal, and shortly had wolfed down the hash and were prowling further into the city.

Trace saw the policeman first. He was walking in a tight little circle around a shattered telephone pole, waving his revolver and talking loudly to nobody. Trace sneaked up within a dozen yards before the cop spotted him. The first bullet cut his ear and the second missed, and then Trace had the gun. He tried to subdue the policeman but the poor devil was hopelessly mad. Trace shot him mercifully in the head. He took the cartridges out of the leather belt and dropped them into his shirt pocket and stuck the gun beside the alien's weapon in his belt. He and Bill Blacknight traveled on, going methodically from street to street in search of recruits.

When dusk came they had six more people. Bill told Trace that it was the damn silliest-looking excuse for an army which he could imagine. Trace shrugged. "They're human, anyhow."

"Are you sure?" Bill asked him. "Even Slough?"

"He has two eyes," said Trace, "and that's the only qualification a man needs for my army."

Slough might be called a midget. He stood exactly four feet high. He was beautifully proportioned, smoothly muscled and lithe-looking. He had a large head with a wild mane of yellow hair, and his eyes were pure Delft blue. He spoke in professorial tones and appeared entirely unaffected by the fact that his left arm was broken below the elbow. Trace set it for him, expertly and swiftly, while Slough talked quietly and with six-syllable words of the ghastly doom he hoped to see visited on the alien destroyers. He said he had been an airplane designer. He was without doubt the most intellectual member of Trace Roscoe's forces, and the only one save Bill Blacknight the magician whom Trace felt he could trust.

There were two girls, red-headed Barbara Skye who had been a secretary and couldn't seem to stop saying how awful, how awful it all was; and a dark-haired woman of twenty-five or so, who had not said a word thus far. Trace believed she was sane, but stunned into a sort of walking coma. He did not therefore consider killing her in mercy, but took her along as a potential ally.

The other three men, all office workers, looked useless; but Trace was setting out to avenge his world, and he had to accept every scrap of manpower that came his way. The three were in various degrees of shock, the worst being Johnson, who wept and shivered if you looked at him, the next Kinkaid, a plump balding man with a bad case of shudders who kept trying to run away from the little band, and the best Hafnagel, almost as big as Trace, with a tic in his cheek and fingers so rigid with nerves as to be almost useless. Johnson had had a rifle when they found him, a heavy sporting thing with four loads that he'd picked up in the rubble of a firearms shop. Trace had taken it from him and given it to Bill. Johnson had been too frightened and sick to protest.

Trace sat them down in a circle on the highest point of what had been the city, where tumbled buildings and upheaved earth made a barren hill which would never produce anything, flowers or homes, for a thousand years.... He stood among them and began to talk. His manner was that of a sergeant with a detail of raw recruits.

"Okay. There are seven of you and by and large I've seen better material, but you'll have to do. Now I'll tell you what we're going to do. We're going to find the green lice that did this to our country, and blast 'em. We're going to make 'em wish they'd never left Venus, or Mars or wherever the hell they sprang from."

Hafnagel, the big man with stiff hands, said something unprintable. "How, you jerk? How can you fight a flying saucer?"

Trace gave him a look that in its time had crackled the enamel on the teeth of many a GI. He said slowly, "My name is Sergeant Roscoe and I am your commanding officer and you had better remember it, Mac, or you will have cause to wish you had become extinct some years before you ever laid eyes on me. Now I shall continue. The fleet of enemy ships left here at a terrific pace between one and two o'clock this afternoon, heading in the direction of Washington, D.C. I haven't spotted one since. Therefore what we will do is pick up our flat feet and head for the capital. God knows what we'll find there, but it's a cinch we've got to get out of here plenty fast."

"Why?" asked Kinkaid, the fat one.

"For one thing, Mac, they'll not be back this way, because what have they got to come back for?" asked Trace patiently.

"All the more reason to sit right here," said Hafnagel. "We can dig enough out of the ruins to live like kings."

"Ignoring the fact that you are gonna go where I say you're gonna go," said Trace through his teeth, "let me ask you, Mac, to take a sniff of the breeze."

"The smell's bearable."

"It will get worse. By this time two days from now it'll be enough to suck the guts out of you. I needn't say why."

"Oh," said Hafnagel, his cheek twitching. "Oh, I hadn't thought—"

"Exactly. Don't try to. Just listen to me. I am your superior officer, Mac," said Trace, "and with you and these other slewfooted remnants I am going to put a crimp in them Martians—*those* Martians—that they'll feel clean to the GHQ. Now we'll take ten and be on our way. I want to clear this area before the atmosphere gets serious."

He looked at them, seven shivering people huddled from the cold into the coats, scarves and parkas they had managed to snatch before their universe had erupted into nothingness. Despair was unknown to Trace

Roscoe, but a grin of wonder touched his mouth; wonder at his own temerity. He was leading these poor reluctant untrained slobs against a million or two giant bird-footed interplanetary warriors, and with about nine-tenths of his mind he expected to do some damage to them. The other tenth said to him, with the voice of his grandmother, "Och, Trace boy, it's mad you are, mad clean through to your Irish bones."

"Wirra, Grandmither," Trace said to her in his head, "it's the bloody English in me too, d'ye see, that won't let me stop sluggin' and won't admit I can be whupped; and then there's all the American of me, and ye know fine that an American never is whupped at all, at all!"

He chuckled—first time that day—and sat down to examine the alien's pistol by the flare of his lighter.

CHAPTER IV

There was a good-enough moon. They made the outskirts of the city by eleven o'clock. A restaurant, all but demolished, gave them canned food; Trace had to bat Johnson in the chops to keep him from wolfing down a dirty chicken sandwich he found lying on the floor, and Johnson went into a fit of wailing hysterics, but when he came out of it he was just about cured, and didn't weep or shiver any longer. They walked a little farther and at midnight Trace plunked them down on a wooded hill, beyond the rayed area. He and Bill Blacknight gathered dry brush and built a blazing fire against the chill of January.

"Dangerous?" queried Slough, the tiny man.

"Calculated risk," said Trace. "I think we can presume the saucers won't be over this sector for a while, and if they do come, they may believe it's a natural fire. The main reason is to attract survivors to us." He didn't mention that he himself was so inured to climatic changes he would never have thought of building a fire for warmth, save for the others. He wore his heavy shirt and trousers and over them a light topcoat Bill had found for him. He could not have said off-hand whether he was cold or comfortable.

When they had all gone to sleep, some like corpses and others as light-slumbering as wildcats, Trace walked a beat around them, keeping an eye and an ear open for approaching steps. There were none.

Toward morning he heard the dark girl sobbing. He sat beside her and stroked her hair soothingly. When Bill took the watch, Trace fell asleep with one arm over the girl's shoulders. At dawn she was all right, and could talk again.

Her name was Jane Kelly and she'd been a teacher, and Trace considered her a very fine-looking dish indeed, even in the fat parka. She was not so flamboyantly female as Barbara Skye, the redhead, but she was distinctly not the sort you would take for a boy at forty paces. She had curves and a warm face and eyes like brown gold, if there was such a thing.

Trace said "Yo," like John Wayne was always doing in those Old West pictures about the cavalry. "Let's travel." They tramped off toward Washington.

They never reached it. They never even got as far as Philadelphia.

The first trouble came as they were crossing a field of frozen mud and corn-stalk stubble; Barbara turned her ankle and sat down with a squawk. She was wearing high heels, not spikes but a good two-and-a-half inches, and Trace was disgusted with himself for neglecting his job. He was so full of vengeance and hatred that he forgot to check on the little things that could sabotage him. He should have scrounged some shoes for her somewhere yesterday.

He glanced at Jane's feet. She wore sensible shoes. They didn't improve her ankles any, but they couldn't spoil them either. Trace had never been an admirer of sensible shoes, yet now he felt a rush of affectionate gratitude to Jane for wearing them.

"You can't go barefoot," he said to Barbara, who was chattering petulantly and rubbing her ankle, exposing an astonishing length of silken thigh in the process. "And you can't travel in those things. You'll have to be carried."

"Why don't you leave her?" said Kinkaid, the plump man. "She's no use to you. Neither am I. I'll stay with her."

Barbara said venomously, "I'd as soon be stranded with one of those bird-footed weirdies as with you, Tubby. Take your cotton-pickin' eyeballs off my leg before I scratch them out for you."

Hafnagel, the big man, said, "Take a vote, Roscoe. You can't force us to limp all over creation with you. Because you're crazy enough to want to find the saucers is no—"

"I'm no soldier," said Johnson. He was a blond man with a crooked nose and jughandle ears. "I'm going to take to the hills. The aliens are invincible; but a man might avoid them for years in the hills. There's farms and such to live off."

"Don't think I'll go with you," said Barbara, standing up. "I wouldn't trust one of you creeps if Roscoe was out o' sight. I'm going with him if I have to walk on my palms."

"We're not splitting up," said Trace. "Someone's got to carry you, honey." His breath misted out on the frosty air. "Hafnagel, you're big enough."

Hafnagel knelt down. Barbara straddled his shoulders, the man took her ankles carefully in his stiff fingers, as impersonally as if they had been firewood, rose and started forward. "Hey," Barbara said, "this is okay. You can see from up here."

"Any saucers?" asked Trace.

"No. Nothing moving at all." They all went on.

Trace's troubles multiplied through the day. Of all his crew, only three were interested in cracking back at the destroyers—the midget Slough, the magician Blacknight, and the teacher Jane Kelly. Barbara was against his plan, but would not leave Trace, whose uniform gave her a sense of security. The three others fought him constantly, with words and sometimes with action.

Hafnagel tried to knock him out during a halt. Trace presented him with a bloody nose, and saddled him with Barbara and drove them all onward.

Johnson broke for cover when they passed a willow-bordered river. Trace caught up with him and washed his face in the icy current, and Johnson restricted himself to verbal attacks thereafter.

Kinkaid refused to budge from their noon camp. Trace grabbed his left ankle and dragged him over the hard rocky earth for twenty yards, and Kinkaid shrieked that he'd walk. Later he pretended to go lame, fooled Trace into half-carrying him for a mile, and then had his fat face slapped so hard that he was filled with respect for Trace's authority, and made no more trouble.

Those were the intentional oppositions. Trace had likewise to contend with recurrent hysterics, with terrible fits of moaning agony of mind, and with a depression that now and again settled over the entire company. He bellowed at them, shoved them around, occasionally patted them like dogs; he realized what they were going through, and he was not a callous man, but he knew he had to keep them on the move for their own sakes as well as that of his plan. Civilization had all but died yesterday. He couldn't expect to pick up a gang of hard, angry, level-headed companions. He had to make do with what he had, and improve on this weak raw material by his tough, high-handed methods.

Again and again he examined the strange firearm he'd taken from that green beast with the flag. It baffled him. There was no place to load the thing, no jointure in all its smooth dark surface. The muzzle was pierced by a hole about a millimeter wide. That was where the missile would come out; but could the weapon be reloaded there? What kind of ammo would go into a millimeter opening?

The pistol—he decided to call it that—was much lighter than a Colt of comparable size. There was a narrow trigger and trigger guard in the same position as on an earth-made revolver. That was logical, as the hands of the aliens were, barring the color, perfectly human. Trace decided he'd have to take a chance and fire the thing. The unchancy weapon would come in handy if he could work it. He bit his lip. Maybe it had just one shot. Oh, blazes. He had to find out.

On their next halt, he aimed it at a tree (there was no sight and he aimed by feel, like a gunman) and pulled the trigger. It had a hard pull, so hard that only a strong man could have budged it at all. It made no sound. There was a thin streak of green light, and the trunk of the tree commenced to smoke and steam. Then it burst into yellow-green flame and exploded, fragments of bark and splintered wood showering out to a great distance. Trace ducked, let up on the trigger, and the beam died. He was reasonably sure now that it wasn't a one-shot.

"And that's what you want us to go against," said Johnson. "A million Martians armed with those. What right have you to make us?" he shrieked. "What authority?"

"This authority," said Trace, hefting the pistol. "Likewise the supreme authority of the United States Army, as I have declared martial law. And then there's the authority of me, Sergeant Trace Roscoe, who will mop up this whole damn valley with your fat puss if so be it you are disinclined to obey my orders, buster."

"Thinks he's so tough," grumbled Kinkaid.

But they all followed Trace when he marched on. Jane Kelly kept up easily with the men, and Trace was especially proud of her; but he had to admit that most all of them were whipping into shape better than he'd any right to hope for. "Few more days and I'll have me a real fine belly-achin' fighting-mad platoon here," he said to himself.

Unfortunately he didn't have a few more days. He made contact with the green-skinned destroyers no more than half an hour thereafter.

CHAPTER V

They lay on the crest of a hill. Before them was a rolling plain spotted with patches of old snow. A thousand yards from the base of the hill was a small town, with figures moving among the houses. It had not been blasted by the saucers, but Trace's people did not run down the slope toward it, because along that plain from horizon to horizon rested a line of the great green spacecraft; and the moving figures, there was little doubt, had olive skin and horny bird-feet and a single eye apiece.

"Reconnoiter," breathed Trace. "Got to know what's what. That place must be local GHQ, and they look dug in pretty solid. I'm going down after dark and give 'em a squint. I'll take Bill with me, in case I want to bring back souvenirs."

"I'm rather more insignificant in the dark than he," said Slough quietly. "And you ought to have three on the party."

"Your arm would slow you down."

"It would not," said Slough firmly. Trace looked at him and after a moment shrugged. "You're right, I could use another." He took the sporting rifle from Bill and gave it to Jane Kelly. He offered the revolver to Slough, who refused it; he handed it to Bill, keeping the alien's pistol for himself. Then he drew the teacher off a short distance. "Look, miss," he said earnestly, "I want you to keep these inter-office-memo types waiting here for me if you can. I don't expect you to actually shoot 'em, but maybe the rifle will cow 'em some. They aren't what you'd call blood and guts sort."

"Why don't you let them go?" she asked suddenly. "What good will three cowards do for you?"

"You never know. I figure they are human, and in the long run they'll show it. Hafnagel is the best—if he has time to recover. He lost his wife in the city."

Jane said, "I was lucky. I hadn't anyone to lose. Except mankind."

Trace looked at her steadily. "At another time, Miss Kelly," he said, "I'd like to tell you what a hell of a fine female you are. I know it wouldn't mean anything to you now, but I must say you are one swell dish." Then he blushed all over his big hawk-nosed face, and turned abruptly to the saucer-cut plain.

In the first darkness the three of them crawled over the top and headed down the slope.

The greenies kept no guard of any kind on their headquarters town; nor, so far as Trace could see, did they set a sentinel over their saucers. They were horribly sure of themselves, sure of having crushed the highest race on this planet. The night was nearly black, thick jetty clouds obscuring the moon, and stabs and splashes of orange light showed where the aliens walked. The three earthmen made their way to the edge of town, took a road straight toward the center, and trotted down the sidewalk past silent houses. They were cautious, but even so they nearly ran into a greenie who came round a corner not twenty yards ahead. They went to earth under a hedge and watched him walk by. The orange illumination was explained: from the front of the helmet he wore, a beam of strong undiffused, red-yellow light shot out and down, showing him the path as he walked with bent head. Luckily he did not flick it from side to side, or he must have seen them crammed under the hedge.

When his soft padding footsteps had died, the midget Slough said urgently, "Trace, do you intend capturing one?"

"I might at that. Why?"

"If you do, remove his helmet at once. Immediately!" His breath mingled frostily with Bill's and Trace's. "The triple prongs atop the helmet may be antennae, for radiating and receiving waves, either of thought or a form of radio. It may be thus that they communicate, so knock off the helmet at once if you attempt a capture, or if we're discovered."

"You are a shrewd cookie," said Trace thoughtfully. "Okay, will do. Now let's get the lead out."

The town had been a small place, with one drug store, one theater, half a dozen stores. The men prowled all round the heart of it, and Trace said, "Here's something funny. They haven't shown any curiosity—the theater's still locked up tight, like it must have been on Sunday when the attack was made on the cities. How come? Don't they want to check on what a building like this is used for? They don't seem to have pried into much of anything."

"Maybe they're not interested in us," said Bill. "Maybe they don't give a whoop for what we've done and how we've progressed. What if they considered themselves so superior to us that they thought we had nothing to teach them? Then they wouldn't pry into our heritage and culture. They'd just obliterate us."

"And why bother to obliterate us?" asked Slough.

"Lot of answers to that," said Trace briefly. "Meanness, desire for sense of power, what have you. Let's nail one and drag tail." He led them past the movie house, and gestured at an orange light approaching. "That one."

"Don't forget the helmet," urged Slough.

"Take it easy, Mac," said Trace huskily. They went to ground behind evergreen shrubs on the lawn of a funeral parlor.

The tall creature neared them, his horny feet with their heavy pads making little noise on the cement. He passed, and Trace launched himself at the broad back, feeling joy wash through him in a heady wave at the first action since his attack on the flag-planter. He struck the alien with all the weight and power of his two hundred pounds, expecting it to pitch forward on its face. It did nothing of the sort. It staggered one step, stiffened, whirled on him. He clutched wildly for a grip, but the stonewall character of this great beast had thrown off his timing. The thing hit him in the face with a forearm. Trace reeled back and fell into a pine tree.

Bill Blacknight leaped on the one-eye even as Trace was hurled away, and darting up one long arm, the magician hit the helmet with the tips of his fingers. In a flash the dexterous hand found the edge of the metal and flipped upward; the alien, squawking, reached for the headgear, just too late. It clanged on the sidewalk. Bill wrapped himself around the steel-tough torso. He knew nothing of brawling, but he was as slippery as an oiled eel. The green man groped for him and he was somewhere else. Terrible hands groped to tear his head from his body, and Bill was a human cummerbund, folded around the waist of the thing and punching desperately for a vulnerable spot. Then he had flattened up along its back and had a half-nelson on the thick throat.

The greenie drew his weapon. Bill did a contortionist trick and booted it out of his hand.

Trace climbed out of the pine tree, swearing bluely.

Slough appeared just before the alien, who tensed his arms to grip the tiny man. Slough was no more than three feet off, well within reach and full in the glare of the fallen helmet's lamp; yet the one-eyed marauder did not catch him. Bill had forced him to his knees. The huge round eye glared across at Slough, while the thing appeared to wait for something unguessable to happen. Slough swung his good arm and caught the brute a healthy crack on the jaw. With a bird's cry, high and ferocious, like the wail of an eagle who has sighted on a rabbit and seen it turn into a wolf, the greenie jerked his head back and staggered to his two-toed feet.

Trace came in like Joe Louis at Tony Galento. He put a fist into the rigid belly and it smashed in like so much well chewed bubble gum. Then he pasted the alien in the throat, pulling his punch just enough so as not to shove the spine through the nape of the neck. Last, as the alien was toppling over, he unleashed the left uppercut which had won him seventy bouts in two years. The greenie flipped up his face and stared sightlessly at the black sky for an instant, whereafter he crumpled into a heap that would never get up and walk away under its own power if it lay there till the crack of doom.

The three friends panted a little at each other.

"Swell captive you have there," said Bill at last. "A lot he'll tell you, Sarge. I heard eighteen distinct bones bust when you biffed him that last one."

"Have to catch another," said Trace irritably. "Damn!"

"And here it comes, at the double," said Slough.

A light bobbed a block away. Bill gestured at the fallen helmet. "Look at that, a regular searchlight." The beam was reaching up to flicker on low-hanging clouds. Its source of power must be startlingly potent. Trace picked up the helmet and settled it on his own head, where it dropped and rested heavily on his ears. He stepped behind a maple tree between sidewalk and street. "Out of sight," he growled at the others.

The second alien slowed, walked briskly, faltered, stopped. He called out a couple of questioning syllables in the avianlike tongue. Trace came out from behind the tree and shot the orange beam directly into the single great eye. In the second's grace he thus achieved, he stepped up to the creature and clipped it sharply, competently, on the button.

"That does it," he said with satisfaction. "We got it made."

He knelt, removed the helmet, passed it to Slough. Then he took off the one which he himself wore and gave it to Bill. "Toss them someplace where the light won't show. Can't mess around trying to turn 'em off—and they might be a couple of booby-traps. Broadcasting stations with brims, that'd lead the enemy right to us." He heaved up at the greenie's middle. He whooshed with surprise. "Little help, Bill," he grunted. "This thing weighs about three hundred!"

With the magician's aid he stood up, holding the alien over one shoulder. He looked toward the invisible hill; he was thinking of Jane Kelly. It doesn't matter a damn about the others, he thought, not even the girl Barbara; but that little teacher with the sensible shoes....

They went up to the theater and turned the corner and there ahead of them were many ducking, bobbing orange lights. A ragged line of aliens were approaching the town, had already cut them off from the hill. They ran, Trace heavily with the inert weight on his shoulder, and there were more coming at them from the other side, so that their only escape lay through an alley that ran beside the theater. Down this they pounded, Trace cursing the helmets which must have shot out warning signals when they were removed; the aliens were coming too fast and purposefully for it to be accidental.

The alley debouched into another, but this was spotted at the ends by more head-lamps. Bill felt a cold touching him that was deeper and more icy than the January wind. He said, "The movie's the last bet," and jumping to the back exit of the place, he performed a swift sleight-of-hand that every magician knows of, and the lock swung open, the hasp flipping back from the staple. He pulled at the door, Slough crept into the blackness, and Trace, still carrying the unconscious greenie, followed. Bill closed the door behind him. It was possible that the extraterrestrial marauders did not know the principle of the padlock, of course; in which case they might not notice the unlocked door. But Bill rather doubted it. So did Trace.

CHAPTER VI

Trace carried the feebly stirring alien along the aisle of the deserted theater, the others following behind him. He went up the stairs to the balcony and found the entrance to the projection booth; negotiated those narrow steps and dumped his captive unceremoniously on the floor between the two big projectors.

"No lock," said Bill, examining the door.

"The place is a trap," said Trace irritably. "Damn it ... but there wasn't anyplace else to go." He knelt and rolled the green man onto his back and slapped his face hard. The alien opened his great eye dazedly, stared round at the three earthlings, and croaked, "What occur?"

"English!" gasped Bill.

"Sure," said Trace. "I expected it. Their emissary learned it and must have broadcast it to 'em while he was being taught. The helmets, the helmets. It's logical."

"Chwefft is told English," said the green man, "we talk English all." He put a hand to his head, and his tight mouth was drawn open into an oval of surprise. "Hat?" he said uncertainly.

"The first one beamed it to the fleet," agreed Slough. "That makes our job easier."

"How?" asked Bill.

"Knowledge, boy, the acquiring of knowledge."

The green man made as if to get up. Trace shoved him back. The creature came away from the floor at him like an enraged panther, striking up with little skill but immense strength at his head and chest. Trace dodged through the perfunctory guard and belted him on the nose, then, as his struggles merely increased, let him have a left cross high on the cheek, just grazing the rim of the eye. The alien cringed and held up his hands in supplication.

"Lousy fighter," said Bill.

"If you think so, I'll time the two of you for a couple rounds," said Trace savagely. "He's scared of his eye being touched; it must be sensitive as hell. Besides, we've got two of those pistols of theirs now, and he's no fool."

"Allow go," said the man on the floor. "Not keep."

"First you talk," said Trace, trying to keep basic English. "How many of you are there?"

"How many? Ah," the thing said, giving a curious one-eyed frown. He had no hair on his head and only a bald ridge for an eyebrow. "*How many* indicating number?"

"That's right."

"Not knowing word for how many. More than you," he said, "more on voyage than you, and more more at home."

"Home? Where's home?"

"The system Lluagor, home planet Chwosst," said the other, sitting up cautiously and clasping his knees. He smiled. His expression said clearly, If these insignificant mites want to question me, what harm can it do? Trace, fighting a surge of Irish rage, went on. Bill prowled over to the openings that showed the deserted theater, squinting through the gloom. They had turned on the lights in the projection booth, and that worried him, for the searchers might come in below at any minute. He found the house lights and threw them on, so that the booth would not glow a warning. Thank heaven the power plant's still working, he thought. As Trace hammered at the green man with questions, Bill began tinkering with the machines.

Bird-foot was saying, in his unpleasant tones, "How many saucers about twenty to forty thousand, this worked out by our mathematicians Chwefft and Hlamnig after learning your system of numbers. Interesting primitive system without knowing sub-space and lacking even name for *fpiolhesit*."

"Sub-space!" exclaimed Slough, darting forward until he stood directly before the alien. "How did he learn the name for that concept, I wonder? But it makes sense. Certainly it would seem logical that such an advanced race would have conquered the mathematically-conceived sub-space, in order to travel interdimensionally from galaxy to galaxy. How else could they go distances that even at light's speed would take a portion of eternity?"

The green man eyed Slough, his head cocked. "Intelligent," he croaked. "Come closer." He reached out a finger that was crooked as if to beckon, bumped it against Slough, and recoiled, an expression of dismay fleeting over his hard features. Then the olive-green skin smoothed out. "Ah. Small, small man. Not know."

"You got a looney," said Bill.

"He's not crazy," said Trace. "I had that sort of figured out before." He left the subject as Bill frowned at him, quite uncomprehending, and said to the alien, "What do you want here?"

"Your planet."

The words were rasped out without emotion, but they were as cold as the wind of January that played outside the theater. Trace said, "Why?"

"Need worlds. Chwosst long ago full, more worlds needing." He labored ahead, perfectly in command of the English he knew, seeking now and again for words beyond his ken, substituting others that were yet clear to the enthralled listeners. For five minutes he talked, and eight and ten, to the three humans in the projection booth; outside his bird-footed, one-eyed compatriots padded the empty town, whose inhabitants they had eliminated with the handguns that morning, down to the last dog and canary. Now they had found the dead alien and the two helmets, now they sought those who squatted in the theater; beyond the town lay the ravaged country, and across its face stretched the lines of thousands upon thousands of quiescent green saucers, some spied on by other survivors of humanity, others proud in a total destruction wrought by their all-shattering rays. Of all of this Trace Roscoe was aware, and still the story of the captive green man pinned him without movement to the closing trap of the theater. Once he thought of Jane Kelly. This thought he battled down, because Trace Roscoe was engaged in a war, and he couldn't have any personal dreams at all....

Gradually the queer speech of the world-assassin painted the portrait of his race, his mission, and his egocentric soul.

CHAPTER VII

So long ago that there were no words for the incredible period of time that lay between then and now, the planet Chwosst, fourteenth from the sun Tsloahn in the star system Lluagor, had become overcrowded to the point of danger. The dominant race of Chwosst were the two-toed one-eyed green men who called themselves Graken, which signified The Mighty, or All-Consuming. The other races of life on the planet were insignificant, small rodent-like beasts used for food by the Graken, who were wholly carnivorous.

They conquered the principles of space travel and sent out fleets of ships—these early craft were bullet-shaped, much as the designers of the first potential rockets of Earth had shaped their creations—and within a hundred-year space they had perfected these so that travel was negligibly dangerous. In their own system they had discovered one other planet capable of supporting their kind. This had given them a long breathing space, during which they hammered at the locked gates of the sub-space corridors. The Graken bred fast, though, too fast, and their two planets filled up before they had solved interdimensional travel.

There followed a long spell of civil war, revolutions that cut their numbers down fantastically and at last came near to exterminating the Graken entirely. While they were repopulating their double homelands, they made a peace among themselves that was never again broken. To assure it, they invented the headgear which broadcast their thoughts, and in a generation or two they had become a kind of ant horde, billions of individuals conditioned to a kind of community thought, a way of life in which every idea of every individual was passed on to those near him, shared and refined amongst so many thousands that a giant race-mind at last made its appearance, and no single Graken ever felt that *he* had conceived anything, but that *they* had done it.

This conjoint cerebration did not reach through space from planet to planet, and so the single-mindedness of the Graken was kept on its track by constant emissaries from one half of the race to the other.

Now a new terror arose for them: the rodents on which they had fed, a breed of beast even more amazingly fertile than the Graken themselves, were decimated by a plague; and nourishment became so scarce that extinction was threatened. Of course there were no rich and poor among the Graken, no money and no privilege, any more than there would be among a queenless ant tribe. So as one grew hungry, they all did. They might have fed half their people and let the other half starve, but that was not the Graken way.

Now, at this most crucial time of their history, the secret of sub-space was finally discovered, and the relatively simple manner of intratime interstellar journeying ascertained.

Patrols were sent out in the old-style bullet-craft, but due to a lack of manual maneuverability in entering and leaving the galaxies now opened to them, the casualties were nine ships out of each ten sent out from Chwosst. Even so, another habitable planet was found within a matter of a few Earth-months, and food (composed of the "inferior races" found thereon) brought back to the hungry system of Lluagor.

The saucer-shaped spacecraft were developed and fleets, so numerous that each of the three worlds became hardly more than a vast landing-ground, were built. Two of every three able-bodied male Graken were trained as pilots, navigators, technicians and attack-masters. Patrols of from ten to fifty thousand ships left the base planets regularly, cutting through dimensions of sub-space in a search for new worlds that was of necessity haphazard, and yet which regularly discovered habitable globes in the limitless reaches of the universe.

No instruments had ever been developed by the Graken with which to ascertain the facts about a planet from a distance greater than a few thousand miles. Thus, to check on size, gravity, atmosphere, animal life and so forth, the patrols were forced to scan a world from just beyond its limit of attraction. One possible haven out of each hundred thousand planets checked was an excellent average, one in half a million more than usual. Some worlds accepted were smaller, with less gravity, others had certain differences atmospherically; but the Graken were an adaptable breed, and readily conformed to such changes.

The one male Graken in three who was not taken for saucer duty became a shepherd, a breeder of food animals, or a scientist.

The females bred and raised their offspring and bred again; their fertile life extended over the years from fourteen to eighty-five, their gestation period was four months. The race was prolific.... The need for worlds was continually urgent.

And Terra was an almost perfect duplication of the Graken's prototype home planet.

The last development in the Graken's marauding through the reaches of space was the actual kidnapping of the new worlds, the theft of entire planets and their transportation through sub-space into the star system Lluagor.

This had been conceived and perfected only a few generations before. The chain of Graken-inhabited globes had reached the sum of fifty-three, and travel between them had become tedious, arduous, and sometimes dangerous, for the ships used for ordinary traveling were fewer and of older patterns than the patrol vessels. The Graken found their communal minds drifting into widened channels, as direct contact became less and less. The pressing need was for a single system of worlds ranged about one star, in which travel would be easy and frequent. They therefore devised the kidnapping principle.

First every planet unfit for Graken life in the system Lluagor was exploded, leaving only two balls spinning about the sun Tsloahn. Then, one by one, the new Graken planets were brought through sub-space and dropped into the home system. This was done by a method which could not be made completely clear by the captive green man; the basic idea of which, however, was easy to comprehend:

A patrol of no less than 20,000 saucers was brought within a mile of the world's surface. They hovered in lines, opened file, linked up until the planet was girdled by one continuous belt of ships. On a planet of the Earth's circumference, this would be about one saucer per mile. The ships were connected electronically in series, and at a button's push, a lever's throw, or a dial's setting in the control vessel, the saucers together with the captive world were shot through sub-space and into the system Lluagor, where they were fixed in an orbit around the parent star Tsloahn. The saucers then drew off, and the Graken owned another world, a new home for their waxing, fruitful hordes.

After two failures, in which planets already crawling with millions of Graken blew up while entering sub-space, the method of annexation was perfected and the remaining forty-nine planets were added to the first two, Chwosst and Csenfar, in the home system. Later acquisitions were brought to the base after any intelligent native races had been crippled or annihilated, and there, in the comfort and convenience of their own spaceways, the Graken mopped them up and settled on them, keeping alive any species that made acceptable food. The journey through sub-space and the orbit-fixing did not affect the atmosphere or inhabitants of the planets in any way.

Thus far, no humanoid (or Grakenoid) races had been found in all the explored universe. The possibility of humans as Graken-food was left undiscussed. Cannibalism, even of this off-beat kind, might be repugnant to the green folk, even though race-murder, of a second-cousin breed like Man, was not.

The patrol fleets were not in touch with their home base, as communication through sub-space was impossible. This was established by repeated questioning of the alien prisoner, whose name was an approximation of the syllable Glodd.

Only chance had brought the patrol to the Solar system. It was so far from Lluagor, even by the dimension-cutting sub-space, that it might never have been found except for an accident in their navigation.

Terra had been conquered and ravaged and would now be kidnapped because of a slip of an alien finger on an unknown instrument panel!

CHAPTER VIII

"Well," said Trace, sucking in his breath, "there *is* some hope."

"Where?" asked Bill Blacknight with deepest woe.

"Tell you later. Did I hear something out there?"

Bill jumped to the apertures and peered into the lighted theater. "There are half a dozen of 'em coming up the aisle," he said. "We are sunk."

"Not yet. What's that film on the reels there? Is it the main feature or a short?"

Bill gave him a glance that said he was out of his head, but obediently pulled the negative out a little and squinted sideways at it. "Feature. All ready to run. You want to entertain these lousy green hellions, Trace?" He shook his head. "My Lord, of all films to show 'em. *The Rise and Fall of the Third Reich.* I saw that eight years ago, and it stunk then—about three-fourths of it's old newsreel clips."

"I know, I saw it," said Trace impatiently. "I noticed the marquee outside and I've been thinking ... can you work one of those gadgets? Those cameras?"

"The projector? Hell, yes. I can do anything in show business. You want sound too?" Bill, mystified, was trying to take orders without thinking about them.

"Yeah. Better start now, I want that ready to run as soon as we get a lot of greenies inside." As Bill began working over the projector, Trace scowled and did his best to remember the Grade C thriller he'd been conned into seeing so long ago. If only he was right about the opening scene! Slough, at the view-holes, said, "They're crowding in. The lights must suggest our presence."

"Get the show on the road," snapped Trace. He stood up; and the alien Glodd, seized the opportunity, rose as though he were spring-propelled and leaped for the stairs that led to freedom. Trace snatched at him, snarling; the Graken hit him with the flat of one big hand and Trace was hurled clear across the tiny room and into a stack of film cans. The one-eye slammed open the door and vanished down the steps, croaking like a buzzard in pain.

"Roll it!" yelled Trace at Bill. "Roll it! And throw up the sound as loud as you can, or we're stew for their supper tonight!"

The ten seconds were an eternity; then it was suddenly a chaos of noise in the theater, a crash of artificial thunder breaking out of nowhere to engulf the startled green men who choked the aisles and searched among the seats of main floor and balcony. Even in the projection booth, where the sound was muffled, the effect was that of some dreadful cataclysm. The thunder merged into a titanic roll of many military drums, and Trace barked, "House lights down!" but Bill Blacknight, the old showman, had already flicked them low.

On the screen appeared a countryside, through which a broad highway cut straight from the camera's position. Far down the road something moved, growing slowly and menacingly as the drums tattooed. The aliens were held petrified, staring with their great single eyes at the panoramic screen and the black and white picture thereon. Even Glodd had halted at the foot of the booth's steps, gazing immobile across the heads of his closest companions, all laved and assaulted by the strange burst of sound.

race stood in the open door, looking at their erstwhile prisoner. Glodd was their worst danger for the moment. There was no telling how much of their conversation about the movie he could have understood; yet even if he'd grasped none of it, he was still the only Graken who knew where they were—and he was not stupid. Trace had one of the ray pistols in his hand. Risking everything, he centered it on Glodd and hauled back the stiff trigger.

Glodd puffed into steam and fire without a sound.

Not one greenie turned his head to see. Not an eye flickered from the giant screen.

Trace prudently shut the door, and jumped for the nearest aperture to watch the movie unroll. Bill had managed to lift the volume of the film even higher, and like a hymn to pandemonium, a paean of ear-shattering vociferance, the drums roared from the screen. Now the movement on the two-dimensional roadway was closer, and the front ranks of countless marching soldiers could be seen. It was an old film clip, taken in Germany at least seventeen years before: Hitler's legions, goose-stepping grandly toward the cameras of a world then—however uneasily—at peace. The soldiers grew, widened, shot higher as they neared. The drums remained like endless thunder, and with them there now lifted the for-long-hateful marching song of the Third Reich.

The green men broke. They fled toward the front of the theater, croaking and squawking, and without doubt their thought-radiating helmets flung the fear and panic from one to another, filling the hall and passing through space and metal into the lines of saucers that lay across the continent and the world. At the front door they were jammed into a struggling mass; someone with a hold on himself thought of using his pistol on the locks, and the wave of green erupted into the dark street.

There was no firing at the screen. The soldiers there had grown to quadruple human size. "Giants!" whispered Bill to himself. "They think they're giants!" Then aloud, over the racket from the screen, he said to Trace, "It's like those natives of India or wherever the hell it was, who ran out of the movie houses to get away from the locomotives that were ramming out at 'em from—"

"It's better than that," said Trace. Once more Bill felt that the sergeant wasn't telling something he knew; but again he shrugged and let it go. Trace was a smart boy and what happened from now on was up to him.

The Graken in the balcony had all tumbled and hurtled to the bottom; the last few stragglers were pounding across the small lobby, uttering their birdlike cries of fear. The German Army was enormous on the screen, now their bootsoles showed huge in the goose-step, now the song and the drums were almost unbearably stentorian. Trace Roscoe grinned widely as the first letters of the title and credits flashed out to an empty house. "Come on," he yelled, "hop to it, you two. I'd guess we have ten minutes to clear this town, before the saucers rip in after the bunch of Goliaths we unleashed on 'em." He laughed as they made for the steps. "First time the Nazis ever did anything good for anybody!"

CHAPTER IX

They did get free of the town, but only just in time. The saucers came in very low, over the heads of the scurrying men, and the rays that lanced out of their bellies were phosphorescing yellow-green. They struck first at the theater, from which until that instant Trace could still hear the roaring of the sound track; then they began leveling the place from end to end, and if their weapons had been atomic, explosive, or any other known military projectile short of a javelin, then the fleeing humans would have died in their tracks. As it was, they were knocked off their feet time after time, were flung headlong to pick themselves up bruised and shaken. But close as the rays came, the men suffered neither concussion nor burns.

Sergeant Trace Roscoe admired the things from his viewpoint as a professional soldier. They were the ultimate weapon if you wanted to destroy an objective without any after-effects, or if you had a pin-pointed target you had to smash individually from its surroundings. The rays annihilated anything they touched, dissolving metal, pulverizing stone, boring even into the ground beneath, while leaving everything beyond the vaporized area inviolate. The Graken were some boys at the scientific business.

Some distance from the town they found it easier going, as the vibrations of the earth were less. They scrambled up the slope of the hill and stood together at its crest, watching the town disappear in green smoke and yellow flame. Then Trace heard, faint yet plain, a sharp cough among the greater noises. Rifle shot! He oriented himself fast, and ran in the cold darkness toward the place where he'd left Jane Kelly with four others and a rifle. For the first time the soldier in him was unimportant, the mission of revenge forgotten, while Trace Roscoe worried over a girl.

He needn't have fretted. She stood squarely on her excellent legs, cradling the heavy gun in two fine long hands, an expression of utter determination on her beautiful face; and opposite her in the murky night sat Johnson and Kinkaid and Barbara Skye, moving nothing but their mouths. Jane, oblivious to Trace's approach, was saying, "Wiggle a foot, anybody who wants it blown off...."

Trace quietly laid an arm over her shoulders, and despite her control she jumped; he said, "Good girl. Damn fine girl." It was the only speech of love he'd ever made, and it didn't sound quite as strong as he'd wanted, but she smiled up at him with relief and maybe a bit of affection in those dark eyes. "I lost Hafnagel," she said then. "I'm sorry, Trace."

"It's okay. Did you kill him?" He saw nothing incongruous in that idea. She blinked and said, "No. I shot to stop him but he dodged out of sight."

"The saucers," squealed Johnson. "They're attacking us."

"They don't know you're alive, Mac. They're smashing the Nazi Army." And he was damned if he'd explain *that* crack, he thought. "Now listen to me," he went on, talking in his sergeant's voice to these reluctant recruits. "We don't have any too much time left. We did something down there that's convinced the Graken—the green ones—that there's a race of giants on the earth. They're blotting out a regiment of the giants, but they are sure to believe there are more. So they're going to want to kidnap this planet as soon as they can, so they can get reinforcements from their base for the big fight." Quickly and untechnically he told them how the Graken annexed worlds for their growing system in some far galaxy. "That may happen in the next ten minutes, or it may take a day or so for them to link up their chain of saucers. I'd say at a wild guess, we have an hour to bollix up their plan. So we're going to attack the saucers—"

Kinkaid screeched indignantly. "What! When we could head for cover—live off farms—hide out in the hills—"

"Get this through your miserable skull," bawled Trace. "If so be it these bastards manage to get us into their home system, we will end up in one of two ways: we will be hunted down and slaughtered like vermin, or we'll be caught and bred for food! There won't be any such thing as guerrilla warfare against 'em. They can let loose a billion or two of their people on every continent on the world!" He stepped close to the cowering plump Kinkaid. "I tell you," he hissed angrily, "I think we have a chance to beat them even now. It has to be fast and it'll take every ounce of brains and every last muscle in this whole damn crew to do it. Now take hold of yourself, you excuse for a man, and remember that your breed—not your state or your country or your nationality, but your *species*—has been slaughtered by the millions; cut down, maybe half wiped out; and now it's heading for the finish, and we're probably the only ones alive who have any idea of the future at all! For God's sake, man, *be* a man! Come on and fight!"

Kinkaid stared at him, his eyes round and frightened in the darkness. Then he drew a breath they could all hear plainly as it rasped in his throat. "All right," he said. "You tell me what to do and I'll do it."

Johnson nodded. "I'm sorry. I don't mean to be scared," he said to Trace. "I'll try to help too."

Well, doggone, thought Trace with satisfaction, I figured they could be made into a fighting force, and so they have been. Doggone.

He briskly shared out the weapons: the revolver to Slough, the rifle with its three remaining cartridges to Johnson, a ray pistol to Bill and one to himself. Then without another word he led them down the hill toward the saucers, which were resting again in their long quiet line beyond the smoking ruin of the town.

Jane Kelly he kept close to him, helping her now and then down a bad stretch of rough, icy ground. Once she asked him, "Trace, why do you think they'll take the earth away so soon? Why have we so little time?"

"Logic. They haven't any reason to wait. They're afraid now of the mythical giants. They'll want to yell for help. And—" he paused, and then with surprise he heard himself telling this woman something he had never said to anyone else. "I'm half Irish, half pure black Irish, and I haven't exactly the second sight, mind you, but I do get hunches and they do pan out. Sometimes I'm all crawling with hunches. Well, I am now. I get the feeling that time's closing down like a goddam—pardon me—like a big steel bear-trap on us. My spine prickles and my flesh is inching around on my bones. It's awful danger we're in at this minute, Miss Kelly, worse than it's been till this minute. My God, maybe they're setting those dials now, and us fiddling around on a hillside!"

"Have you any hunch about whether we'll beat them?" she asked seriously, and a feeling of awe at something unknown in his voice took hold of her. He was phrasing his sentences like a wizard in a bog, and she could almost smell the incense of prophecy.

He growled something that sounded obscene. "No," he said, "I tell you true, I haven't the least idea of that. I only know we've been given a peep at their secrets, and if we don't foul the Graken, nobody ever will." Then he leaped down a steep place, and was silent.

CHAPTER X

As they ran with loping strides across the frozen plain, Trace heard a shout behind him; he turned his head and there was Hafnagel, pounding after them and calling desperately. Trace slowed a little, jogged on until the big man had caught up with him. "I thought you lit out for the thickets," said Trace shortly.

Hafnagel panted. "I decided to throw in with you," he said. "I was lying out in the brush listening to you.... I was lonely." He waved his hands, groping for an explanation for conduct he did not wholly understand. "You're crazy," he said, "but I have to go with you. A fellow's got to strike back, I guess. He can't take everything lying down."

"Come on," said Trace.

They neared the first saucer, which lay, a colossal green metal eye staring up at heavy clouds in the winter sky, quiet and yet aware. Bill Blacknight said, a crack in his voice, "Are they looking at us? Are they watching us, Trace?"

"Dunno. We're going inside. Remember, once a Graken sees us, the whole bloody tribe of 'em knows where we are. We've got to kill instantly, or knock the helmets off before we're spied, understand?"

"But a helmet sends a radio message when it's removed," the midget Slough protested. "Those helmets called the aliens to them—"

"I doubt it," said Trace. "I think they're useless without a Graken head in 'em. Each of those beauties had a second or so in which to think *danger, danger*! Now let's find the way into this hulk." He turned away impatiently. There was no time to argue possibilities. There was only time to act, and maybe there wasn't even that.

Swiftly he completed a full turn around the silent spacecraft. He could see nothing that might be an entrance; the green metal, steel or whatever alloy might be tougher than steel, showed no crack or crevice. Lord, he thought prayerfully, Lord, we have to find it fast.

Slough said, "It must be one of the ports. Check the ports." He gestured to the rim of the saucer, a thick border which widened every thirty feet to make an oval opening; these were perhaps two feet deep, and closed there by a smooth plate of metal which Trace presumed would slide away in time of need, to allow guns to project or possibly to serve as rocket jet exhausts. The openings would admit a man, all right, even so large a man as a Graken. And if one of these was the door, then it must be openable from the outside.

He set his group to checking each port; but Bill Blacknight stepped back a little, his mind buzzing. If I was a green one-eyed bird-foot, he thought, and I was trotting up to my personal saucer, I wouldn't want to peer closely at every damn port on the rim before I found the door, would I? Hell, I'd want some sign somewhere, a pointer I could spot without any trouble. Where'd it be? Near the top, most likely, and it ought to be plain enough to see without squinting. He examined what he could see of the top of the ship. The center was a raised bump, round and wide. Bill felt his mouth twitch up with excitement as he saw that it was not a perfect circle; off to the left it pushed out into a sharp point, as though the circle were being pierced from within itself by an arrow. He ran to the section of the edge to which this indicator aimed, and found one of the ports directly in line with it. Softly he called Trace, who came at the double.

"This is it?" asked the sergeant. "Can't see any difference. How do you figure?" Bill told him, as he scanned the lip of the oval port for signs of a door. Nothing. "Boost me up," said Bill.

Hafnagel held him on his shoulders, and Bill leaned into the port and ran his educated fingers over the smooth surfaces therein. He found the lock, a raised set of thumb-sized nodes and two bars that would not move for him. Frantically he searched his mind for every trick he knew of locks and bolts and all such mechanisms. He began trying various manipulations, all his years of magic concentrating in the flying fingers.

The metal plate slid without sound into the sidewall, leaving an opening through which a diffused green glow poured out into his face.

Bill thought of the peculiar way he had moved the node and bar, and node and bar.... In all the world, it was not likely that any man except a trained magician would have touched them in the right sequence. He puckered his lips and whistled without noise. "What if I'd studied for the law, like Mother wanted me to?" he murmured. "Holy cats!"

Taking the initiative, he hoisted himself from Hafnagel's shoulders and wormed into the hole. The passage was slick without being actually greased, and within seconds he rose to his feet in the first room of the great disk.

Trace followed, then the others, Hafnagel coming last. They gathered in a taut, apprehensive group, staring about them.

The room was empty of life. There was no sound in the saucer save for their own quick breathing.

CHAPTER XI

Without a glance at the curious furnishings of the craft, Trace Roscoe headed for the door on the right-hand side. It was a tall rectangle, like an earth-made door, but without knob; as Trace came within a foot of it, it slid into the wall so briskly that he would not have touched it had he been coming at a dead run. Electric eye, or the same principle, he thought, striding forward.

Nor was there anyone in this room, which was plainly a sleeping chamber. Trace marched for the next barrier, but Slough darted over to investigate a narrower door, and thus discovered the first two Graken. The vanishing portal showed a lavatory, and the pair of greenies stared up, startled, from a massive washbowl, in which they had been bathing their faces and bare arms. Their helmets were slung on wall pegs. Both of them went for their pistols, but Trace, not so surprised as they, beat them to the draw. He fired over the tiny man's shoulder, and the Graken died, their flesh dissolving into steam and fragments.

Barbara Skye said her first word in an hour. It was triumphant, but quite unprintable. Jane Kelly said nothing, but she grinned at the other girl with appreciation.

Trace bethought himself of the old Western axiom, that one good man with a rifle was worth four good men with revolvers. He took the big sporting gun from Johnson, and, thrusting his ray pistol into the front of his shirt where it would be handy, walked purposefully at the next door. He had a feeling about this one.

He wasn't wrong. Three aliens grouped around a table, bending above some chart or mathematical calculation, turned and rose as he stepped into the doorway. Two of them he blasted before they had glimpsed him, and the third he took in the face with a heavy slug just as the beast was opening his mouth to shout or challenge. The rifle echoed like artillery in the small room, and Trace thought with a momentary despair that it had likely been heard all through the ship. He stepped over the twitching corpses and went on.

This time the door opened before he had neared it, and a green man, ready and tensed, stood on the threshold with a gun in his big fist. Trace, caught for an instant unawares, went to his knees and jerked up his pistol; it shot its deadly thin stream of force on the heels of the alien's, and he saw it strike the broad chest and begin to disintegrate the whole being. The Graken's shot had missed.

Well, it had missed *him*, Trace realized, as he heard the sharp gasps behind him. He looked and saw Kinkaid's headless body topple over between Barbara and Jane. It proved the incredible depth of the women's feeling for this fight and this terrible problem, for neither of them screamed....

Shoulder to shoulder Trace and Bill Blacknight went through the room and their pistols' beams snaked out without sound together, as before them the control panels and intricate machinery of the pilot cubicle appeared behind three tall green-skinned Graken. Slough's revolver bellowed hoarsely behind them. Bill felt a tug at his coat, and later discovered that a great patch of cloth had been burned away by the enemy's rays. Johnson, half-crazed with anger now and gone quite berserk, plunged past them as they fired at the aliens and the last spitting stream from a pistol caught him in the belly and burst his body asunder.

They were in the control room, the six who had come this far alive, and the door through which they had leaped would not close. Bill fumbled wildly at the jamb, at the edge that was flush with the wall, and then Slough said, "The bodies! Roll away the bodies!"

Hafnagel and Bill took unpleasantly blasted corpses by the heels and dragged them out of the cubicle; then, having cleared the space near the door, it slid swiftly shut, leaving them outside. They went to it, it opened, and at last the six were together in a shut room.

Trace handed his pistol to Hafnagel. "Can you trigger it?" he asked, thinking of the man's stiff fingers. Hafnagel put out his hand and flexed it easily. "Don't ask me why," he said shortly. "It happened when we came into this thing." He took the weapon.

"Nervous release," said Trace. "I've seen it happen under fire." He turned to the bank of mechanisms, the sprawling panels full of controls. "Brother," he said under his breath. Then he went to work, trusting the others to guard his back.

Even when he heard Slough's revolver bang twice, he did not look up from the things he was working on.

CHAPTER XII

They had killed nineteen Graken, and Slough, reloading the clumsy revolver with his tiny hands, presumed that the entire crew was not dead. They had killed nine on their way in here, and had finished off ten more since, as they barged in the door or crept up to it to attack the presumptuous humans.

The queer part of it was that, although Trace had been sweating blood over the instruments for more than a quarter of an hour, no reinforcements had appeared from the other saucers. Slough did not understand this. Certainly a number of those perishing Grakens had sent out frantic messages for aid before they died; and according to the late Glodd's story, such thought-calls should have been heard even over in Europe, Africa, or Asia, let alone in the saucers that were, so to speak, just next door.

The only answer seemed to be that one saucer was expendable. This, considering the Graken's mutual reliance, must mean that every other saucer was engaged in work of the utmost importance—such as forming the chain which would carry Terra through sub-space into the system called Lluagor.

He handed his revolver to Jane Kelly. The girl was pale, but her features were set in strong, determined lines. Slough admired her; she was one of the finest specimens of womankind he had ever seen. "I don't think we can expect more visitors, my dear," he said to her, adding to himself, *unless we find ourselves in another galaxy*. "You keep this ready, however." He went to Trace Roscoe.

Trace gruffed at him. "Don't need you. Get back there."

"Of course you need me. I was an airplane designer, remember? I have some knowledge.... Have you found the electronic device yet?"

Trace turned up a lined and agonized face. After a moment he said, "No. Not yet."

"Keep going, then. I'll start at the other end," said Slough.

The banks and panels were far more intricate even than they had first supposed. Slough believed that the device they were searching for would probably be a type of klystron, considering the ultrahigh-frequency application. Whatever turn the Graken science had taken, he felt the the principles of electronics, being universal, must be those involved in this sub-space travel; and it did not seem reasonable that an electronic mechanism could be very different on Chwosst or Terra or Mars or any where else.

Trace believed this too. He was a pretty fair student of electronics and he doubted that any race could disguise a high vacuum thermionic tube or an amplifying circuit or a thyratron so that he, Sergeant Trace Roscoe, couldn't identify it. The photoelectric cells that opened and closed the doors seemed to be of the same type as those used on this planet for the same function; Trace had taken two minutes off to pry off the cover of the cell in the left wall and inspect the construction. So he ought to know the "kidnap-device" when he came across it.

He glanced at his watch. More than half an hour had passed since they entered the ship.

The race of man hung on his fingers, which fumbled among a myriad esoteric gadgets in search of one which might be no more than a pair of resonant cavities, an anode, a cathode, and a grid. He felt his coolness departing, the sweat of terror stood on his face, he lost the tough-sergeant veneer and became a panting, panicked man.

Then he caught the eye of Jane Kelly, and he bit his lip and told himself off in Gaelic cuss words, and went to his job again with a firmer grip.

And in five minutes he found the device he was hunting.

"Slough!" he shouted, in the bull's roar that once had nearly drowned out the Red guns in Korea. "Slough, come here!" And the small man, who had been six steps away, bounded to his side with his blue eyes wide in astonishment. "Is this it?" asked Trace fiercely. "Am I right, is this it?"

Slough glared at the small recess, and said, "Aha!" It was an intricate and highly specialized form, if he was any judge, of the resonant cavity magnetrons with which he had worked often in the past. He said so, and Trace nodded. "Okay. Now we gimmick it."

"Can I help?" asked the midget, eager as a boy.

"You're damn right. My fingers are too big to get into all the crannies. You do what I tell you; get in behind the tube, like so, with your index finger...."

As Trace ordered and Slough obeyed, the others came round them, still alert for raiders, but eager to listen to the mysterious words which came, sharp and intense, from the sergeant's lips. Now and then Slough would disagree, and they'd argue; Bill began to fidget with apprehension. The words were Greek to him.

"But if we lead in the wire from this other thing, which has got to be the fuel feed—"

"Why must it be? We don't know it is. I say build up the frequency of oscillation until—"

"Well, then, stick your damn fingers over here and hold this steady while I—"

And so on. Bill was certain that it would never end, that they must be caught at sunrise by an investigating party of the green aliens; but suddenly the midget and the soldier were moving off from the control banks, looking at each other with expressions half smug and half fearful. "Let's get out," said Trace abruptly.

"What did you do?" asked Jane Kelly, as they hurried through the rooms toward the entrance port.

"Gimmicked it," said Trace. His hand fell on her arm and squeezed reassuringly. "The electronic device is now altered so it'll build up an intolerable frequency; it's also connected with the thing we think is the fuel feeder, and with a row of buttons we're almost certain connect with the blasting rays."

They reached the port. "In other words," prompted Jane, "what?"

"In other words, when the ships are set to zoom old Earth into the sub-space subways, this disk is going to blow sky-high; and since they're all connected in series electronically, the whole goddam fleet will explode simultaneously."

They wriggled through the short passage, dropped to the ground. It was very dark on the plain. Patches of snow on the ground showed dark shapes of tree and bush and boulder; after the green light of the saucer, this outer world was dim and full of illusions. Jane thought she saw a Graken approaching, and stifled a scream when she realized it was the shadow of a swooping owl. She said loudly, "I don't like it."

"What?" asked Trace. They were standing in the shadow of the saucer, indecisive.

"I don't like this. It's too easy. It's a let-down." She grasped him by the arms, and he, startled, looked down into her face that was a lovely softened blur in the night. "I'm half Irish too, Trace Roscoe, half pure black Irish; that's the Kelly in me. And I tell you plain, I feel wrong about this. It can't happen so pat, you can't just change a wire or two, hook up this and attach that, and foil the kidnapping of a whole world. There's something wrong, there's a thing missing that's vital."

"Baby," he said, so low that no one heard but the girl, "I can tell you what it is. It's a security on this. Because there's about one chance in a thousand that what we did will work like we want it to. That machinery's out of this world. Half of what we did I can't explain to myself, even. We just made a purblind stab at bollixing the deal."

"It's something else. You're forgetting something. Oh, Trace, Trace," she cried suddenly, gripping him savagely in her anguish, "I know! It's that there's no crew in this saucer, and they aren't coming to fight us! That means they've either taken the earth into their galaxy already, or else that they'll do it without bothering about this saucer—and then where will your fine plan be?"

Trace almost sat down, his body went so limp. "Oh My God," he said slowly in capitals. "I never thought of that."

"You've got to get a crew here," she said, as the others crowded about them stammering their worry and terror. "You've got to get them out of their ships, no matter how busy they are, and let them see that they can take this one over again. They can't know anything that's happened since we killed the last one in there."

"She's right," exclaimed Bill. "We have to create a diversion to suck 'em out of their hidey-holes, Trace."

"The only way is to attack the saucers," he said wearily, "and how we do that with two rayguns and a revolver, heaven only knows."

"Why, we do it with two rayguns and a revolver, then," said Barbara suddenly. "Why not? That next saucer's maybe a hundred feet away. Take a shot at it, for Pete's sake. Try it and see."

Trace inflated his chest and stuck out his jaw and once more he was the complete sergeant. He tore the pistol from Bill's hand, raised it and sent a streak of green death arrowing at the dark bulk of the spacecraft. Playing it along the rim, he tried to strike the oval ports with it; and he did not release the trigger for a full minute. "Now let's see," he said. He looked at Jane and the redhead. "You two take off," he barked. "Head for the hill, pronto." His tone was so unanswerable that they ran, Jane twisting her head back at every third step. Shortly they were out of sight.

Nothing moved, and if there was any damage to the other saucer, it could not be seen from where the men stood. Trace, impatient, was lifting the weapon again, when a green light shone out from the center of the edge.

"Ah," breathed Trace. "We've raised 'em. Now let 'em come, don't stop 'em, and we'll man this death-trap yet!"

CHAPTER XIII

They lay in a kind of shallow ditch just under the outer edge of the great saucer, watching the orange lights from the helmets bob and duck nearer. Bill said quietly, "We're cut off from the hill now."

"That's okay. The women will wait; and we can fall back on the ruins of the town if they chase us. They may just investigate the ship here, and not bother with us. We are only vermin, after all."

Hafnagel said, "What if they see the changes you made in that panel?"

"They shouldn't, unless they look almighty close."

"And will it work?" asked the big man.

"Who the hell knows?" retorted Trace irritably. "Maybe it's too late now. Maybe we're spinning around Tsloahn already. Who can tell? We can't see the stars, the clouds are too thick."

The aliens were very close now and the four men fell silent. The lamps drew up to the deserted ship, hesitated, and at last one lifted and disappeared, as its wearer vanished into the open port. Trace shut his eyes and said a quick private prayer of thanksgiving; then he whispered, "We're okay now. Let's head for the ruins." They crawled out of the ditch and like a quartet of raiding Comanches, their work done, made for the empty wreckage at top speed.

Behind them a shout went up, a raucous croak of triumph. Then a voice said weirdly in English, pitched high and carrying, "Not run, die!"

Trace got the idea, disagreed with it, and put all his strength into a terrific sprint. He found himself bathed in orange radiance, as the distant Graken focused their helmet beams; just before the first green ray was fired, he saw a very low wall of bricks miraculously uncrumbled, jinked and made for it, dived over and landed on his chest with a scarce-felt smack of pain. The others followed him, and hugged dirt as the rayguns sliced the cold air harmlessly.

After a while the orange glow went away. Trace cautiously looked over the wall. He couldn't see anything but he had a feeling. They hadn't all gone into the ships, he knew that.

He was not quite unprepared, therefore, when the Graken came over the bricks on top of him.

It was probably the largest and heaviest of all those whom the band had seen. It fell on Trace like the side of a collapsing barn, and Trace felt all his breath leave his lungs in one excruciating wheeze. He fought to bring the muzzle of the raygun against it, but could not move his arm, which was pinned under the creature's knee. Only the soldier's left arm was free. He flailed a blow that landed solidly, but the alien only squalled, and chopped at his face with its clubbed pistol. Trace felt skin and flesh give way along his cheekbone, blood gush from the slice of the metal. He heaved up as heartily as he could, at the same time aiming another left jab for the brute's face. His knuckles took it square in the eye. It shrieked, reeled back on its knees, and Trace fought tigerishly and was free. He delivered his finest right cross to the throat, and the Graken writhed on the frozen earth. Then Slough and Bill were there—the fight had taken only seconds—and the magician in a frenzy of rage booted the green head with the toe of his heavy shoe. That was that.

Slough's voice said softly, *"Monstrum horrendum, informe, ingens, cui lurmen ademptium."* He rolled the big head up to the dusky light, and the broad single eye gaped blankly. "Virgil said that about another Cyclops, luckily of a mythical breed. 'A horrible monster, misshapen, vast, whose only eye had been put out.'" He signed. "Trace, the only real work we had is done, for failure or success it's finished, and we can't do any more good here. Let us go back to the women. If so be it our plan succeeds, they'll need you to watch over them in the—ah, the post-war world, which may be a little wild for a time. And if we've lost our gamble, then you should be with your girl when the end comes. You can't do any good by fighting guerrilla-fashion down here."

"My girl?" asked Trace, who had no idea of how he had been mooncalfing at Jane Kelly.

Hafnagel laughed. It was a joyous sound, the expression of a troubled man who had found release. "Go on, Sarge," he said. "Go to the hill, all three of you. I'll cover your withdrawal from here." He hefted the raygun he carried. "Don't argue with me," he said before Trace could speak. "You know a retreat needs a rear guard—and I mean to have another Graken scalp or two before I quit. Go on."

Trace argued in passionate whispers, but shortly found himself creeping on all fours across the razed town, without fully remembering how he had left the wall. There was no sound or sign of movement on all the wide plain; and as they came to the beginnings of the slope, he said, "I shouldn't have left him. He ought to have come with us."

Then they saw in the distance the streaks of green fire, and a pair of orange spotlights which almost immediately went out. The ray pistols kept darting their beams along the ground, and Trace said again, "I shouldn't have left Hafnagel."

"He never meant to follow us," said Slough.

"It was right to leave him," said Bill Blacknight quietly. "You gave him a few minutes of glory. That's no bad deal, you know."

When they crested the hill, the green shafts had vanished, and the plain was dark under the heavy clouds that hid the sky.

CHAPTER XIV

The five of them sat on the lip of the hill, hunched up against the cold, clasping their knees and occasionally rubbing hands or ankles for warmth. Trace had one arm around Jane Kelly, whose dark head lay against his chest. He was almost happy. He thought he had lost, lost his vengeance and his universe, and still he was all but contented, because he had this girl close to him.

The saucers rested without motion on the plain. The clouds had thinned, the moon's location could be told by its misted radiance, but no stars shone and the humans could not tell whether they were spinning around Sol or Tsloahn. After all, as Trace had said, the moon might have been kidnapped with them—or it might be a different moon, one of the other stolen planets in the Graken's home system.

Barbara hated stillness. She asked Trace, "How come those greenies thought your damned old movie was real? Couldn't they tell it was only a picture—them and their high IQ's?"

"No," said Trace. He roused himself and looked over at her. Bill Blacknight was snuggled against her (oh, for warmth, sure, thought Trace cynically) and the magician was obviously on the verge of the same strange happiness that touched Trace himself. "No," he said again, "they couldn't tell it was a picture."

"Why not?"

"Because they only have one eye apiece."

"I don't see what difference that makes."

He assumed the role of patient instructor, dredging in his memory for the right words. "You need two eyes functioning as one organ to have what they call binocular vision. The retina isn't adapted for three-dimensional perception, see?"

"No," said Barbara.

"Well, to perceive solid things for what they are, you have to have two retinal images, thrown on both eyes by the one object. You get help from linear and aerial perspective—if you know the size of a thing you can judge how far away it is—but supposing you don't know its size, you're liable to misjudge its distance if you've only got one eye. One eye, two dimensions; two eyes, three dimensions."

"I get that," said Bill sleepily. "How'd you happen to think of it, Trace?"

"It was Slough here. Twice a greenie made a mistake as to how far away he was: once on the street, when it didn't grab for him when it could have, and again in the theater, when Glodd motioned for him to come closer, and hit him accidentally. Both of them thought Slough was average human size. Both were looking at him from a low viewpoint, the first on its knees and Glodd sitting on the floor. That's when it occurred to me that their eye-sight must be two-dimensional. Of course it wouldn't bother them on their home planets, where everything was known by size and aerial perspective filled in their deficiencies. Probably their navigational instruments made up for their lack of depth perception in flight, too. But when I turned the Nazi Army onto them, they were baffled. They must have thought giants were coming up out of a hole under the theater. Which is why they ran like hell, and then blasted the town."

"Very clever," said Slough. Jane echoed this, and Trace said to her quietly, "I'm not quite the uneducated slob you might think I was, baby."

"I don't think anything of the sort! You're—you're a man, a fine tough intelligent man." She was so sincere she sounded angry. Trace glowed with pride.

There was a very long silence then. Nobody moved from their chosen vantage point. The hidden moon went down. At last Trace cleared his throat self-consciously.

"I'd like to ask a question myself. Of you, Slough."

After a slight pause, Slough said, "What is it, Trace?"

"Well, you're a little too smart a geezer for reality, if you know what I mean. You figured those helmets for thought-radios, when it was a fantastic possibility that no normal man would have hit on so quick with so little to go on. Then you did things with the electronic device in that saucer that I couldn't have come up with in a coon's age."

"I'm an engineer," said the tiny man. He chuckled. "And I read a lot of science-fiction."

"Okay. Then there's this. Thirty-odd hours ago you had a badly broken left arm, which I set for you and put in a sling." Trace spoke slowly, almost with fear now that he voiced his suspicions. "Some time during our first raid on the town, you discarded the sling; when we were in the saucer, you fought and afterwards you worked on the instruments with both hands. It's impossible, but it must be true—your arm knit completely within a day." He turned and bending over Jane Kelly he stared wide-eyed at the dark figure of the little man.

"Slough," said Trace huskily, "*what are you*?"

Slough sighed. "Whatever I am, Trace Roscoe, I am not your enemy. No, nor ever shall be, yours or your people's. Look!" He cried out so suddenly that the four of them, shocked, stared out in the direction in which he gestured. "The saucers," he said, "they're rising!"

"The gimmicked one?" asked Bill, whose eyes were bleary with lack of sleep.

"Yes, all of 'em," said Trace. He jumped up, hauling Jane to her feet with him. "It's coming, they're hoping to do it," he said, and he clenched his teeth and took a firm grip on the girl, as though he wanted to hold her on the earth when it shot into the uncanny regions of sub-space. "Hold tight," he said, with no particular sense but a vast deal of emotion. "Hold tight, Jane baby." And Jane held him tightly.

The saucers rose higher, dwindling in size; they reached the low cloud layer and passed into it, becoming hazy and then invisible.

Twenty thousand spacecraft girdled the globe, linked electronically, readied for flight with their stolen planet to unknowable distances of deep space.

The men and women waited, their breath emerging in brief white frosty spurts in the cold air. And nothing happened.

After twenty minutes, Trace put a trembling hand to his forehead. "We lose," he said. He saw Slough begin to walk away from them, going back along the gradual slope among the bare trees, but he did not even call after him. It didn't matter a damn now, what or who the midget was.

"We lose," he said again, and hugged Jane fiercely.

And then the sky exploded.

CHAPTER XV

Trace flung himself on the ground, sheltering Jane; he felt rather than saw that Bill had done the same with Barbara. He gazed up, and saw the great rack of clouds torn and dispersed by the force of the blast. There was a chain of brilliant green-white balls of light, like so many bursting sky-rockets, that stretched from horizon to black horizon across his world. He thought of the shards of metal, the evil whistling splinters and hunks of meteoring death that would rain out of the sky after such a multiple explosion, and he buried his face in Jane's soft hair, trying desperately to cover her whole body with his own. The noise above them was so mighty a roar that Trace was deafened, and his head hummed and rang intolerably.

In that moment, oddly, he thought again of Slough, and realized what he must be. The Irish intuition, second sight, or what-have-you it works in a cockeyed way, he said to himself, waiting for the shower of molten hail.

Slough was of the extraterrestrials too!

Oh, not the Graken, the wicked green one-eyed bird-footed destroyers. But he was a saucerman, right enough. Lord knew how many of them had been living among us before the greenies attacked. No telling how many had died, how many still lived.

Trace remembered the saucer sightings that had perplexed the Air Force for so many years before. The blue-lit disks that soared and dipped and shot away from pursuit, the disks which had been seen by reputable folk for—well, possibly for centuries. Funny he hadn't thought of it before, but all those well-vouched-for sightings could not have been Graken. The Graken shot into our system no longer ago than late December! And all the long while before we'd been under the surveillance of *blue-lit* saucers—not green, but blue at night and silvery in the sunlight!

He wriggled, his body awaiting the impact of the metallic missiles, his mind occupied with Slough.

And if there'd been saucers here for so long, and even saucer-people among us, what had happened to them when the Graken came? Any space battles between warring saucers would have been seen. Had they retreated to their own planet at sight of the Graken fleet, through space or interdimensional sub-space? Maybe. Or maybe they'd hidden in or on the earth.

Why hadn't they fought? The Graken had no allies in the universe. The blue-disk cowards had run! Except old Slough, if he were one, he hadn't run. Why had the great ships left Terra? Not their fight? Or....

Or suppose they couldn't fight! Suppose they had no weapons in their craft, no rays nor bombs—Trace exclaimed wordlessly as this probable truth occurred to him. The blue disks were only observers, they weren't warcraft. Perhaps their people had no weapons at all. Perhaps they were a nation of peace, as the Graken were a nation of eternal war. And their long watch over the world had been either curiosity, or hopeful friendliness.

In which case, they'd likely be back. Trace hoped they would; he had liked Slough. Terra could use friends now.

He jerked his head up and stared at the sky. Even if the Graken ships had been three miles up, their remains should have showered down to earth by this time. He got to his feet with a grunt. The gimmicking of the controls in that saucer had been better than he'd known; the ring of saucers had not only exploded, they'd been atomized.

Trace helped Jane to her feet, as Bill Blacknight did the same for Barbara. "Well," said Trace, "let's not sit on our cans out here all night. Let's get this show on the road. We have a hell of a lot to do."

"Such as what?" asked Bill.

"Mac," said Trace firmly, "this is still the Army of the United States, and we got a world to police up. There'll be more left than us four; there'll be millions of people, here and on the other continents too, who'll need all the help we can give 'em."

"We can help the world?" asked Barbara. "Us four?"

"We've done a lot already," said Jane drily.

"There's more, we haven't begun yet. We have to find a radio, get in touch again," said Trace, his voice strong and happy. "There ought to be some planes left, in private airports and out in the country. We got to scrape together what's left of civilization and patch it up and make it better than it ever was. You know anybody that could do the job better?"

"No," Jane said, "darling." Trace blinked. He was not a demonstrative man, but he leaned over and kissed her on the nose with haste and embarrassment. "Come on," he said, gulping a little, "we got work to do."

They started off along the crest of the hill, and then Bill grasped Trace's arm and said in a whisper, "Oh, oh Lord, we forgot."

"Forgot what?"

"We may be in the Graken's star system, what the hell was it, in Lluagor! They took such a long time—maybe they got us there before they blew up!"

The four people searched each other's faces silently, and even Trace was too appalled at the thought to verify it for a moment. Then Jane Kelly turned her face up to the sky, where the clouds had been rent and scattered by the blast.

After a long moment she put her hand in Trace's.

"I'm not much of an astronomer, Trace," she said, her voice calm and sweet and proud. "But even so, I can recognize the Big Dipper when I see it." She pressed his fingers affectionately. "And I *do* see it," she said....